Goal Setting

*The 10 Step Method To Becoming An
Unstoppable Goal Achiever*

Brad Jones

Table of Contents

GOAL SETTING

GOAL SETTING

Introduction

How These Goals Changed My Life

Dear Reader,

The book you are about to see isn't meant for an afternoon of light reading. It isn't meant to be skimmed and ignored, or set aside until you feel like picking it up again. It isn't meant to help you determine whether or not you need to set goals in your life. I'm not trying to convince you of anything here. If you purchased this book, it was because you've already (consciously or unconsciously) decided that something about your day-to-day life needs to change.

This book is here to make that happen. It's meant to be interactive. It's meant to be an opportunity for you to change your life by following the same tactics, tips, and action steps that I did when I was younger.

Before I earned a six-figure salary, I was a waiter. Pay was minimal. The restaurant was getting ready to go under, and the owner could only afford to write me a check every other week. I didn't mind, though. It was convenient. I lived right down the street, and I didn't support myself.

I dropped out of college after my freshman year. I was nineteen. I didn't have any aspirations for my life. I just wanted to be a teenager. I never wanted the responsibilities that came with being an adult. I didn't think about becoming anything more than what I was; a parasite, eating away at my parents' savings. I didn't really care.

It was like being in an intellectual coma. Nothing my parents, my friends, or my extended family did or said was able to wake me up. In fact, it wasn't until my parents sat me down and told me that they could no longer afford to support me (tears in my mother's eyes) that I finally realized something had gone horribly wrong in my life.

I had become apathetic to my surroundings; a broken cog in the social system. I didn't want anything more than what I already had. And it was slowly destroying me, and the people who loved me.

I saw a counselor. And, once I was getting help, I started developing this series of steps to creating life-altering goals. Six months later, I was out of therapy. I was back in school, and I was running my own business. Six years later, I'm making more money each year than I ever could have dreamed as a teenager.

I promise you that the methods you're about to be introduced to work. Why? Because they changed my life. And I guarantee, if used correctly, they can change yours.

There's power in a good, strong goal. There's power in something that you believe in. Something that you want more than anything can be the carrot that guides the mule. It can be the difference between being a lifelong waiter or a self-employed entrepreneur. You have to really want your life to change. Otherwise, it never will. And you need to take steps to get there.

After my "awakening", I spent a fair portion of my life attempting to become someone that I would have, as a child, looked up to; and someone that my children will be able to look up to, as well. I feel that I've accomplished that. But it was only after many years of very hard work, and a whole lot of determination.

If you're looking for anything similar to that, you need to read this book.

A letter of introduction wouldn't be complete without a breakdown of what you're about to see. By using this book as your guide, you will:

Determine the aspects of your life that require goal-setting by exploring common problem areas such as physical traits, emotional stability, mental health, financial assistance, employment opportunities, romantic relationships, family issues, contribution needs, education, and organization.

Choose a goal-setting method that works for you by investigating the SMART Method, as well as the Zig Ziglar Formula, the One Minute Approach, and the Agile Approach. You will also be provided with basic goal-setting tips, such as making measureable goals, keeping a timeframe in mind, being clear and precise, writing goals down, and being realistic.

Clarify your desired outcomes by exploring your personal problem areas and determining your needs.

Explore timelines, tips, and important information, such as the difference between long term and short term goals. You will also be introduced to the idea of "timed goals", each involving a separate time period of one week, one month, three months, six months, one year, five years, or ten years.

Set your goals while learning the difference between performance goals and outcome goals, as well as realistic goals and unrealistic goals. You will be encouraged to track your goals and commit to them.

Learn how to stay accountable for achieving your goals by sharing them with family and friends, focusing on the task at hand, remembering that your goals are attainable, remembering that you have power over them, and always being realistic.

Educate yourself in reviewing and evaluating your goals by asking yourself important questions, measuring your progress, and studying your outcomes. You will be able to determine when goals are becoming a problem in your day-to-day life, and when goals have truly become unattainable.

Troubleshoot your goals by studying popular barriers, such as sleep deprivation, hunger pangs, withdrawals, communication issues, outside interference, and unrealistic goal-setting. You will also take steps to fix "troubled" goals by studying popular solutions, such as taking naps, creating healthy meal plans, seeking help or counseling, changing your tactics, or changing your goal altogether.

Change your goals, and create new ones based on the difference between attainability and impossibility. You will ask yourself important questions, such as what went wrong, whether or not a change is necessary, what you can change to fix the "troubled" goal, or whether or not the goal itself is needed.

Take action to change your life by following your goals, using methods such as writing your goals down, talking through your problems, refusing to give up, focusing on the future, celebrating your success, being confident and proud, continuing to track yourself, making more milestones, keeping a planner, and staying organized.

Until this program was created, I felt that my life had no purpose. It wasn't until I learned how to efficiently set goals and make a future for myself that I began to succeed in my own problem areas. I improved my relationship with my parents, I fulfilled my educational needs, and I developed a business that continues to provide me with financial stability.

Now, I'm going to help you do the same thing.

Sincerely,

Brad Jones

Step 1: Determine Your Needs

The first (and most important) step in this process is going to involve taking a good, hard look at your life and determining which parts of it don't meet your expectations.

Do you struggle in your romantic relationships? Are deadlines and procrastination particular problems for you? Do you want to have a better understanding of your emotional health and stability?

In essence, you need to figure out what elements are missing from your day-to-day life. In order to do that, you need to be familiar with the ten categories that you should (in some way) experience or deal with on a regular basis.

Those categories are:

- Physical Traits
- Emotional Stability
- Mental Health
- Financial Assistance
- Employment Opportunities
- Romantic Relationships
- Friendships
- Family Issues
- Contribution Needs
- Education and Organization

Everyone has physical traits. Whether they are comfortable with them or not is a different story. Everyone deserves emotional stability, mental health, financial assistance, and employment opportunities. These are aspects of your life that need to be fulfilled in order for you to stay healthy, happy, and productive.

Romantic relationships, friendships, family issues, contribution needs, education (as in, your ability to do well and retain good grades), and organization are all aspects of your life that are controlled (for the most part) by you. These areas are where most goals are set, because mistakes that will negatively affect your future are often made when you aren't satisfied with your performance in these categories.

In the following section, we'll discuss each category more specifically. You should make a mental note or write down any area that you feel fits your particular needs. You'll want to reference this list in later chapters.

Which Areas Need Improvement?

As you sort through the following traits, you should ask yourself a few questions. Do you feel that you are satisfied with your current standing in this category? Have you made any recent progress in this category that you would like to continue through setting goals? And, even if you don't necessarily need to set goals in a particular area, is there anything you could improve upon that would benefit your future?

For example, I feel pretty confident in my sense of organization. However, there are improvements that I could make (such as purchasing a filing cabinet or hiring a secretary) that would help me, in the long run. These are things that you need to be thinking about as you run down this list.

You should, of course, be highlighting aspects of your life in which you are truly lacking. But you should also look deeper, and think about the underlying problems (usually in the areas of emotional stability, mental health, and financial assistance) that are causing your initial concerns.

I might be struggling with my decision to go back to school. That falls under education and organization. However, I might also be showing signs of depression, which needs to be addressed if my self-confidence is ever going to be high enough to get myself interested in the future of my education. I might also be struggling financially, which is keeping me from rendering a fair decision. Though my problem is located in one category, the causes of that problem are located in others.

Make sense? Let's take a look.

Physical Traits - This includes anything and everything from the top of your head to the tip of your toes. It encompasses a vast number of important identifying factors, like your height, weight, body type, eye color, hair color, nail shape, skin color, clothing size, and foot size. Most often, we hear about discrepancies in our self-confidence related to bodily appearance in the areas of weight, height, clothing size, and skin color. Many parts of our body can be altered with the help of recent scientific discoveries and man-made inventions. Colored contacts allow our eyes to appear a different color than they really are. Nail files and manicures allow us to perfect our nail size, shape, and color. Hair dye allows us to change our hair color on a regular basis. But the categories most often disliked by their owner? These are the parts of our body that are either very difficult to change, or cannot be changed. It's an extremely common, and understandable, struggle for self-worth and dignity.

Emotional Stability - This is anything related to your general mood and how that mood affects the world around you. Having a bad temper, being surrounded by unhappy or unhealthy relationships, feeling intense sadness or frustration, and lacking a sense of overall control when it comes to your emotions, are common problems in this area. Usually, emotional instability is created by other factors in your life, such as bad romantic relationships and friendships, discomfort with your physical appearance, bad dieting habits, or depleting financial assistance. If you feel that your emotional stability is becoming an extreme problem, or you're beginning to worry that there's something more to it than meets the eye, you should seek counseling or speak with your physician. You could be looking at a mental health problem. Most individuals that struggle in this aspect of their lives, however, find that they are generally unhappy and need to alter their thought process and coping mechanisms to better handle their daily life and activities.

Mental Health - Unlike emotional stability, mental health revolves around more uncommon issues, such as depression, bipolar disorder, and anxiety. This is anything that can be diagnosed by a therapist or a doctor. It might require medication. It might require some other form of treatment, such as aromatherapy or counseling. Goals for issues in the mental health area are usually easy to set, but difficult to achieve. Since you're dealing with this problem through no fault of your own, you can't accept blame for it. You also can't stop your body from generating the problem. It's a significant part of who you are. You'll need to find a comfortable balance between working to better yourself through the treatment put in place by your doctor, and accepting that certain parts of your life will be affected by your mental health. If you're looking to practice new habits or coping methods, this is a great target area for you.

Financial Assistance - Financial problems are perhaps some of the worst, and most difficult to solve, issues that we face every single day. They are also some of the most common. Saving money is a hard thing to do. Learning how to budget is a hard thing to do. Being able to say "no" when someone asks you for help is a hard thing to do. However, at any particular point in your life after you've moved out of your parents' home, you should be financially stable. If you're not, goals need to be set to achieve that status. Maybe you need to find a better paying job; one that provides more benefits and maximum hours. Maybe you need to downsize and find a way to live on a more manageable income. There are an endless number of problems in the financial area, but there are also an endless number of methods to solving these problems.

Employment Opportunities - This category encompasses all things job-related. As humans, we thrive on being useful. We latch onto specific fields of study, and we aspire to work in our respective fields as we age. We don't want to be at the bottom of the totem pole for more than a couple of years. We aren't content doing the same thing every single day. It's very unlikely that you've purchased this book, yet you'd be more than happy to work in retail for the rest of your life. You want something more. Every individual with goals and desires is looking for something more. Until you're making quality money for a job that you truly enjoy, you aren't sufficient in this area. There's always room for improvement. Why? Because there are so many opportunities available to us, especially with online developments. Hundreds of job offers are at your fingertips. You just need to know where to look, and how to go about organizing your attempts.

Romantic Relationships - This speaks for a wide variety of issues, such as attachment needs, intimacy issues, a lack of trust, or fear of commitment. Basically, anything that negatively affects your relationship with a significant other (or affects you getting into a relationship in the first place) falls under this category. Are you too busy to schedule dates? Do you struggle with communication? Does your hot temper keep you from dealing with disagreements in a rational, understanding manner? Nearly every human being has the drive to spend their time with another human being. Whether that partner be a man or a woman, it doesn't change the underlying fact of human nature. We need companionship. We crave it. Without this aspect of our lives, we are lonely. We feel worthless. We lose hope for the future. Luckily, goal-setting is a great way to restore your inner romantic balance. We'll talk more specifically about the kind of goals you can set in this category in a later section.

Friendships - Perhaps the only thing we require more dramatically than romantic relationships are friendships. Fortunately, our friendship need can be fulfilled with a single, quality friend. It can also be fulfilled with many quality friends. However, it cannot be fulfilled with a single, fake friend. It cannot be fulfilled with a hundred fake friends. We usually run into problems with our friendships when we discover that we don't have as much in common (morally, ethically, religiously, etc.) as we thought we did. This leads to conflict. Some goals in this area might be set to solve how often you spend time with your friends, how you spend your time when you're with your friends, and what you choose to do financially because of your friends. Again, we'll discuss this more in detail in a later section. But you should keep in mind that a crucial sign of a good friend is one who won't push you into doing something that makes you uncomfortable. If you feel that your friends violate these ethics, you have some improvements to be made.

Family Issues - Family requirements vary among the different generations. In the newest generation (known as the millennials), we find that children are developing strong family attachments. Some of these attachments can become detrimental later in life, when the time comes to move away from

14

home and start your own future. Other attachments have rendered a sense of morality and togetherness that has been unprecedented in previous generations, and will most likely be passed down. You may have goals to set in this area if you find that your family has become too dependent on one another. You may have goals to set in this area if you find that your family has become too independent of one another. It can go both ways, and you need to be able to determine whether or not your relationship with your family is becoming a source of conflict in your daily life. This category also involves improving your overall family connection, if you feel that you've lost it altogether.

Contribution Needs - Some people are perfectly comfortable going through life and focusing solely on themselves. Their needs, their wants, and their desires all become the most important factor. That doesn't necessarily mean that they're wrong or refuse to be empathetic. It's just a way of life. However, other people prefer (or even feel the need) to give back somehow. They feel the need to contribute to society in a useful, remarkable way. You may feel as though your current line of employment or what you choose to do in your free time isn't beneficial to the world around you. That might bother you. That might not bother you. If it does bother you, you are probably struggling with your need to contribute. Popular goals in this section involve volunteer work and community service, donating to a good cause, or helping the homeless. If you're looking to improve your life while improving the lives of others, this is a great additional category to add to your goal-setting strategy. You'll be shocked at how good it makes you feel and how productive it helps you become.

Education and Organization - This final category includes a very large array of things, such as your desire to learn, your need to go to school, your drive while you're in school, and your ability to do your homework. It also involves organizational strategies. If you find that you can't keep track of paperwork, homework, important items or files, gifts, emails, phone numbers, and other meaningful objects, you probably need to improve your skills. I struggled with this aspect of my life, specifically. The basis for any entrepreneur is a quality learning experience and an eye for organizational tactics. Otherwise, we aren't able to successfully start a business, let alone keep the business running regularly. The majority of my goal-setting took place pretty evenly between this category and financial assistance, and it is always my suggestion that new "goa6l-setters" start here. This is the platform for your future, and how you will choose to set your standards. Are you the kind of person who can live with ending your studies after high school? Do you feel the need to attend a university? Is your room usually a mess, or are you nitpicky about its status? These might seem like little things when compared to the other categories, but they actually matter more than anything else when it comes to improving your life.

Your Assigned Action Task

Now that you're familiar with the ten categories of your life, you need to read them again. Then, read them one more time. After that, you should compile a list of **at least three** sections that could use improvement and goal-setting. These are the areas that you'll continue to study and experiment with as you work your way through this book. You can always come back and add more, but choose wisely. Being able to successfully pinpoint areas in which you need help shows that you're serious about setting these goals. And that's where you should be, if you want to succeed.

Next, we'll talk about goal methods and how you can choose the right one for you.

Step 2: Choose A Goal Setting Method

We won't actually be setting goals for several more steps, but I find it increasingly important to inform my readers about different goal-setting methods. Everyone functions differently, and has a unique way of responding to particular situations.

If I tack my goals up on a board, I'm going to follow them. That's just how I work. I don't need much more than that. And, if I find a goal isn't working for me, I make a quick change and push it back into motion. However, you might prefer incorporating your goals into some kind of statement or way of living that puts them together into one, overall concept. You might prefer using technology and electronic tracking devices to monitor your goals.

No matter what option you choose, you should feel comfortable with your goal-setting strategy. You might want to try two or three before making a solid decision. Rather than talking you through this just before we set our goals, though, I want to talk about it now. I want to give you time to think about your options, and maybe experiment with them.

I'm sure you're wondering why. After all, they're just methods, right?

When I first started setting goals for myself, I used a complex series of bullet points and drawn out ideas. One goal would fill an entire piece of lined paper, and then some. I quickly learned that this method was faulty, and that I wasn't meeting my goals the way I'd hoped. The reason behind my failure was simple. I didn't feel comfortable. I was just trying to do what I thought was the most thorough strategy.

I was wrong. And, in being wrong, I wasted two months of my life attempting to meet goals that didn't match my personal standards. If I'd been taught how to set them properly and how to organize them in a way that fit my personality, I would have accomplished quite a bit more. To keep you from making the same mistake, we're going to spend this section discussing some goal-setting tips, and the methods that can make your dream a reality.

Common Goal Setting Methods

In this lesson, we're going to focus on four of the most popular goal-setting methods. These include SMART Goals, the Zig Ziglar Formula, the One Minute Manager Approach, and the Agile Approach. All of these methods have minor differences. In the end, you can choose one of the listed strategies, or you can use ideas from each strategy to develop your own concept of what works for you.

SMART Goals

This is, by far, the most popular way to set your goals. Each of the five letters stand for a different tip that your goal-setting strategy should follow. We'll discuss each of them separately.

Specific – Your goals should be specific to the area of your life in which they are targeted. They should be clear, concise, and easy to understand. You should be able to walk away from your goals for two or three weeks, and still know what they mean when you come back. If you don't make your goals specific enough, you'll find that you're going to have a very difficult time meeting them. Let's say your goal is to "become a better person". That's a great start. That's a wonderful and honorable goal. However, there's really no way to move forward from that statement. How do you decide whether or not you've "become a better person"? You should try something more specific, such as "volunteering at the local recycle center at least six times" or "adopting a puppy from a shelter".

Measureable – Your goals need to be attainable. Going back to our "becoming a better person" statement, you can't determine whether or not that's actually happened. There's no way to really measure that. Whereas, if you pledge thirty hours of your time at a homeless shelter, you can measure that. If you swear that you're going to lose fifteen pounds, you can measure that. We'll talk more about the outcome of measuring your goals in a later section. But you

18

should know before you begin creating your goals that you can't put a value on how far you've come unless you're able to tell whether or not you've actually met your goal in a real and provable way.

Achievable – Some goals are just impossible to meet. No matter what strategy you use to create your goals, you need to be mindful of what you can and cannot do. I always say that a bucket list and a set of goals are two very different things. It's not fair to set a goal for yourself that relies on chance, outside factors, and things that you can't control. For example, saying that you're going to win the lottery isn't a goal. It can very easily be put on your bucket list as something that you would like to have happen to you. But you can't make that an aspiration of yours. You don't have any control over it, other than purchasing a ticket.

Realistic – In the same way that you should pick goals that are actually achievable through your own means, you need to be realistic about what you can expect from yourself. We'll definitely touch on this in later sections, so I'll only give you a brief warning. But setting unrealistic goals for yourself can be damaging to your ego, your organizational structure, and can actually cause you to procrastinate more often. Why? Because you're being constantly discouraged. It's better to keep your sights low and celebrate plenty of milestones, than it is to set the bar very high and never have anything to celebrate.

Time-Bound – You cannot have goals without putting a time stamp on them. It just doesn't make any sense. Our entire fourth step is dedicated to this topic. You can make weekly goals, monthly goals, bimonthly goals, and annual goals. You can try to guess where you'll be in ten years. You can even make lifelong goals that just need to happen before you die. These are all fine. But determining how long it should take you to complete a goal will help you prioritize and organize yourself. And this is very, very important when it comes to taking your goals seriously.

The Zig Ziglar Formula

This method of setting goals can be broken down into seven steps. It's more to-the-point than the previous method, but approaches the same ideas from a different angle.

(1) You should always write down your goals. It proves that you're making a commitment.

(2) Set a specific deadline for your goals. It's easier to quit when you don't have a timeline.

(3) Limit your obstacles. If you don't have internet access, find a local library with a free hotspot. If you need more money, find oddball jobs to get you there.

(4) List your skills and knowledge. This will help you identify what you need to obtain your goals, in addition to what you already know.

(5) Identify your allies. Everything is easier when you have help.

(6) Develop a plan of action. List the steps you need to take and figure out how you're going to take them.

(7) Document the benefits that you'll receive when your goals are achieved. Focus on your reward. It will keep you going.

One Minute Approach

This approach can be broken down into six steps. It's short, sweet, and to the point. It practices concise and swift goal-setting, which works for those who don't have the patience for long, drawn out plans of action. To help you gauge the difference, I started with the Zig Ziglar Formula. I ended with the One Minute Approach.

(1) Set your goals. They should be quick and efficient; no second guessing.

(2) Determine what you should be doing. What is the end result?

(3) Write out each goal, using as few words as possible. You should still be clear.

(4) Read and re-read your goals.

(5) Look at your performance for the next few days/weeks.

(6) Determine whether or not your behavior matches your set goals.

The Agile Approach

This method involves looking at goals from a new angle. It denounces SMART goals and prefers a more realistic approach. If you're choosing to follow this method, you should follow these five tips:

- Goals shouldn't be created to intimidate you. If you can't achieve it, it's not the end of the world.
- Goals shouldn't be created simply to impress other people. This needs to mean something to you.
- Goals shouldn't favor short-term wins over long-term losses. You need to balance the two.
- Goals shouldn't distract you from your everyday life. Rather, they should influence it.
- You should avoid having too many goals. It might seem efficient, at first. But it's going to hurt you, in end.

There are also some important questions that you should also yourself when setting agile goals. For example:

- Is the goal specific and understandable?
- Is the goal simple?
- Is the goal manageable?
- Is the goal attainable?
- It the goal ambitious and stimulating?
- Is the goal relevant?
- Is the goal inspiring?

The most important thing you need to remember about agile goal-setting is that it prefers functionality over ethics. Rather than refusing to set a goal because it doesn't seem measureable, those who use agile goals are going to set it anyway, and find a way to solve the problem.

Tips For Setting Goals

You've been introduced to four popular goal-setting methods. Now, we're going to give you some broad tips that will help you focus each method further. Keep in mind that not all of these pieces of advice are necessary, but they are highly recommended.

Make Each Goal Positive

There's a big difference between saying that you want to be less of a failure this year, and saying that you want to be a better person this year. One implies that you're putting yourself down; that you don't think you were good enough last year. The other lifts you up; it encourages you to be better than you were. This is especially important when setting goals because, without positivity, you aren't going to be encouraged to follow the rules. It's hard to be invested in something that feels like a slap in the face each time you read it. So, rather than asking yourself to be less of an idiot, ask yourself to be smarter. Look toward the future, instead of dwelling on the past.

Set Priorities

We'll talk more specifically about timelines further along in the book, but it's important that you understand the concept of priorities. Without them, your goals will seem meaningless, overwhelming, and confusing. Try sorting through your focus points (family, friends, etc.), and determine which of them are the most important. These goals will be your primary focus, while your next important point will be your secondary focus, and so on until you've reached your lowest priority. Sometimes, how long you have to complete a goal also has an effect on how important that goal is to you.

Take A Firm Stance

If you're going to make a goal for yourself, stand by it. Don't let anyone talk you out of it, and don't second guess yourself. It's one thing for your family or your friends to doubt you, but once you doubt yourself, you'll be facing a whole new kind of problem. You have to believe in yourself in order to set successful goals. If you don't feel comfortable with a goal, or you feel like you might not be able to complete it, don't set it. It's always better to set five goals that you feel especially confident about, than it is to set twenty goals that make you anxious when you talk about them.

Involve Others

They might not have the best reactions, but telling the people you love about your goals helps you remain accountable for completing them. We have an entire section devoted to this, but you should be aware of the fact from the get-go. Goals are more easily attained when there's someone standing by, cheering us on or discouraging us. Those who cheer for us encourage us to keep fighting. Those who discourage us push us to prove them wrong. It's a win-win scenario for everyone. So, when it comes to telling other people about your goals for the future, don't hesitate.

Welcome Failure

Maybe you can't complete a goal. There's nothing wrong with that. It means that you're human, and you've been ambitious about the goals that you've decided to set. Once in a while, you aren't going to make it. That's nothing to beat yourself up about. That doesn't mean that the problem can't be fixed. That doesn't mean that you can never set successful goals ever again. It just means that you need to welcome failure, and learn from it. What would you change, if you could do it over again? What would you keep the same? How could you have altered your goal? These are the things you need to be thinking about.

Use Software

Perhaps the easiest way for "organized" individuals to follow through with their goals is to download special applications to track them. As a technology-driven society, we love the idea that we can connect our Smartphone with our current desire to get fit. We love that we can track how many words we've read, how many photos we've downloaded, and how many text messages we've sent. We're all about statistics. If that's your thing, use software to manage your goals.

You'll find that it feels satisfying to cross off an accomplished goal, and that phenomenon is going to push you to do it even more often.

Your Assigned Action Task

We've spent some time talking about the different types of goal-setting methods, as well as a number of tips to help you throughout the process. Your assigned action task for this step is to choose (or design) a goal-making method that stands out to you. Practice it, with a few mock goals. You'll need it during step five, when we go through the process of goal creation.

Before we get to that point, though, we need to talk about something even more important. How do you determine what your desires are?

Step 3: Clarify Your Desires

We can't even begin to set goals for ourselves until we know what we're looking to accomplish. Before we actually sit down and make decisions that could affect the rest of our lives (and should affect the rest of our lives), we're going to discuss what you might be looking for from each of the categories that we introduced in the first chapter.

By this point in time, you should have picked at least three of the given categories. You also may have come up with categories of your own, and that's perfectly fine. Your job throughout this chapter is to generate ideas about what you might be looking to get out of your goal-setting experience. That's really what we're going to talk about here. What do you want?

The reason we're having this conversation is because many people make the mistake of setting goals without really thinking about the final outcome. They don't step back and consider what they're looking to achieve, in the overall sense of the word. They sometimes only focus on the here and now. What am I getting or not getting at this very moment? That's not the way we want to look at this.

Goal-setting is a way of improving your life, and should be treated as such. That means that the goals you set in the respective categories you chose should reflect an overarching set of final goals. When we say that your goals should be specific, we're saying that they should be branched off of the general goals that we're going to discuss now. These are your fictional finish lines.

Below, we're going to go through each category individually and generate ideas that might encompass what you're feeling. If you see anything that speaks to you, I highly suggest you write it down.

Physical Traits

If you're looking to improve in this category, there's probably something about your appearance that you just don't like. Some examples of broad goals could be:

- I want to lose weight.
- I want to be healthier.
- I want to be stronger.
- I want to be able to take care of myself.
- I want to be different.
- I want to stand out.
- I want to be liked.
- I want people to look at me.
- I want "so-and-so" to like me back.
- I want to feel better about my appearance.
- I want to feel more confident.

These are only a few of the possible examples. There are, of course, many more. But this should give you a general idea of what most people who choose this category are looking to accomplish. Using this, you should be able to write down more specific ideas of your own.

Emotional Stability

This is a more complex category that could include overall goals such as:

- I want to have a better romantic relationship with my partner.
- I want to learn how to control my temper.
- I want to have a better relationship with my parents.
- I want to learn to apologize for my actions.
- I want to learn to improve my range of emotions.
- I want to learn to be rational.
- I want to learn how to interact better with others.
- I want to learn how to control my emotions.
- I want to learn how to be less afraid of the people around me.
- I want to learn how to be happy.
- I want to learn how to be calm.

Most people dealing with emotional problems feel unstable, unhappy, and desperate for a sense of control over themselves. If you feel anything similar to this, you should write down some of the bullet points above and determine whether or not they apply to you.

Mental Health

These goals are usually a bit more pointed than emotional stability goals, with things like:

- I want to learn how to control my anxiety.
- I want to get help for my bipolar disorder.
- I want to learn how to pay better attention in class.
- I want to learn how to cope with my social anxiety.
- I want to reduce my level of panic.
- I want to reduce my panic attacks.
- I want to have less anxiety attacks.
- I want to learn how to control my depression.
- I want to feel happy.
- I want people to like me.
- I want to feel comfortable in my surroundings.
- I want to look forward to the future.
- I want to get help.
- I want to learn how to say no.
- I want to stop hurting myself.

Yes, these ultimately sound more serious because (in a sense) they are. These diagnosable problems take a large amount of work to improve upon, and the road is long. Goals for this category should be set with the assistance of a professional.

Financial Assistance

There are a vast range of goals for this category, such as:

- I want to hold a steady job.
- I want to make more than $15 per hour.
- I want to have benefits.
- I want to be financially stable.
- I want to learn how to save money.
- I want to start my own business.
- I want to support myself.
- I want to better support my family.
- I want to be more responsible with money.
- I want to be accountable for my own future.
- I want to be living in my own apartment.
- I want to spend smart.

The younger you are, the more likely you are to want to include this category in your goal-setting regimen. Why? Because you haven't yet mastered the skills of being a financially stable, self-sustaining adult. You'll be able to work on these goals with a series of short, timely tasks that keep you on track.

Employment Opportunities

Everyone has the right to work, but not everyone is happy where they work. Some overall goal-setting in this section includes:

- I want to be happy in my line of work.
- I want to have a steady job.
- I want to make $20 per hour.
- I want to start a 401K.
- I want to have benefits and vacation time.
- I want to get along with my coworkers.
- I want to be respected by my advisor.
- I want to be liked by my boss.
- I want to be a hard worker.
- I want to be someone that people look up to.

- I want people to be inspired by me.
- I want people to want to be like me.

These very broad goals encompass just a few of the common choices made by those who focus on this category for improvement.

Romantic Relationships

This is a particularly difficult one, because every relationship is different. But, at the heart of our romances, we're all looking for the same thing. For example:

- I want to be respected in my relationship.
- I want to feel happy in my relationship.
- I want to feel wanted by my relationship.
- I want to be compatible with my partner.
- I want to improve my relationship with my partner.
- I want to fall in love with my partner again.
- I want to get my partner to fall in love with me again.
- I want to learn how to be a better partner.
- I want to learn how to have a better partner.
- I want to learn how to walk away.
- I want to learn how to tell the bad people from the good people.
- I want to learn from my mistakes.
- I want to be in a healthy relationship.

Again, there are hundreds of options for this section. But, if any of these ring a bell, snag onto it. You'll need it.

Friendships

Friendships are also difficult. We all choose to be friends for different reasons, and we all choose to walk away from friends for different reasons. But some popular options include:

- I want to have real friends.

29

- I want to be a better friend.
- I want to stand up for myself.
- I want to stop picking on other people.
- I want to be nicer to my friends.
- I want to inspire my friends.
- I want my friends to like me.
- I want my friends to respect me.
- I want to make more friends.
- I want to meet more people.
- I want to "get out there".
- I want to learn how to say no.
- I want to learn when to say yes.

A few ideas can take you a long way in this category, because the number of people you can focus on has the potential to be quite large.

Family Issues

These are rough. Everyone has a complicated relationship with their family. There's no getting around it. If you've chosen this section, you probably have some issues to deal with that can't be solved overnight. Popular overall goals in this category can include things like:

- I want to separate myself from my family.
- I want to improve my relationship with my family.
- I want to learn how to stand up for myself.
- I want to get closer to my siblings.
- I want to be more accepting of my family.
- I want my family to be more accepting of me.
- I want to have a healthy family relationship.
- I want to feel happy around my family.

While you can't fix relationship problems on your own, you can certainly push for effort from others, in order to improve your lifestyle and your future.

Hopefully, they will include themselves in your quest for peace.

Contribution Needs

There are significantly less options for goals in the "contribution needs" category. Why? Because it all boils down to the same thing. Wanting to be helpful. I've spoken with individuals who've said:

- I want to a better person.
- I want to make a difference in the world.
- I want to help my friends.
- I want to help the homeless.
- I want to make the world a better place.
- I want to inspire others to volunteer.
- I want to give more of my time.
- I want to donate more often to charity.
- I want to give someone a home.
- I want to adopt from an animal shelter.
- I want to adopt a child.
- I want to have a positive effect on someone.

There's probably very few things that are more difficult to achieve than changing the world, or making a difference. But there's also very few things that are so rewarding, when you finally manage to succeed. They certainly won't be accomplished overnight, but these goals are worth setting.

Education and Organization

More often than not, this is the category that I suggest to people who are just starting out when it comes to making a place for themselves in society. If you're fresh out of high school or in college, this is the section for you. If you're moving out of your parents' home for the first time, this is the section for you.

It might include statements like:

- I want to be more proactive in school.

31

- I want to get better grades.
- I want to continue my education.
- I want to be more organized.
- I want my life be less cluttered.
- I want to learn how to keep everything under control.
- I want to learn more about basic life skills.
- I want to keep a calendar.
- I want to graduate.

If you don't have the drive to continue to learn, you're going to have a very difficult time adjusting to your new goals. Goal-setting involves a sense of motivation. You have to want it. This category helps you with that particular need.

Your Assigned Action Task

You've been given plenty of ideas. Now, it's your job to write down and specify what broad goals you're hoping to accomplish throughout this process. You'll be using these goals to make your official, more specific, goal sets. Create a list of **at least ten** goals.

Next, we're going to discuss (as promised) the issue of priorities and creating timelines.

Step 4: Create Timelines

Setting proper goals (ones that are going to last) usually require making a set of timelines.

For example, you wouldn't say that you want to write a three-page paper without giving yourself some kind of deadline. Not all goals require these, but the majority of them do. In this case, you would set a deadline of (probably) about a week. If that didn't seem reasonable, you could set it for a month.

Other goals require longer terms. Saying that you want to change the world is a lifetime deadline. You want to do it before you die. Almost like a bucket list item. A goal stating that you want to get into a serious relationship might be set at five years, or ten years.

We'll talk about realistic goals in a later step. But you should keep in mind that certain goals need more time than others to complete. Expecting to jump into a serious relationship in six months is probably not going to be a very proactive decision, on your part. These are things that you need to think about before we set our goals in the next section.

In this step, we're going to talk about the difference between long term goals and short terms goals. We're also going to give a few timeline examples for popular term lengths (one week, one month, three months, six months, one year, five years, ten years, and lifetime).

Short Term Goals vs. Long Term Goals

One of the most important things you'll learn as you work your way through the goal-setting process is that some goals are more "pressing" than others. You'll have to quickly decide where your priorities lie, and how you're going to organize your plan of attack. A useful way to accomplish that is by labeling your goals are either "long term" or "short term".

Short Term Goals

Short term goals are the little changes that enforce the bigger picture. For example, if I'm trying to spend more time with my kids, I'm going to set aside certain hours each week. I'm going to create a series of milestones that I want to complete before I can say that I've checked off my overall goal.

Generally, short term goals are defined as anything less than a year. I don't quite see it that way. In my mind, there's a little section squished between the two categories called "Significant Goals". It's the perfect middle ground between the long and the short.

You probably wouldn't see a three-month goal as a short term goal, right? And yet, it isn't exactly long term either. That's where this new category comes in; to describe those middle points. In my opinion, short term goals are anything that measure within a month or less. Significant goals are anything larger than a month, but smaller than a year. Both short and significant goals make a different in the long run, but they're used in unique ways.

Spending more time with your children is a significant goal. It's not going to take a year, but it's not going to happen in thirty days. Whereas writing a paper is a short term goal. You'll be done within a week.

Long Term Goals

Anything longer than a year is a long term goal. These are meant to keep track of your overall improvement. They are the broad ideas that we discussed in the previous step. For example, if my goal is to have less anxiety attacks within the next year, I'm not going to be able to check that off until my year is up. It's a long term goal.

However, it has many short term repercussions. Theoretically, there could be a weekly goal, specifying that you don't want to have more than two anxiety attacks that week. If you manage that for a year, you'll meet your long term goal.

So, the short term goals enforce the work, and the long term goals make you feel fantastic when you meet them. They aren't just a little check mark on a long list. If you meet these goals, it means that you've managed to do something that, at one time, you didn't think you could do. And that's the point of this whole thing.

Timeline Examples

The difference between long term goals and short terms goals is only one way to split up your ambitions. You can also put an exact deadline on each of them, allowing you to work in one of these subcategories.

One Week

These short term goals are the driving force behind your goal-setting venture. As you constantly check these off your list, you'll feel a sense of commitment and pride. Having many week-long goals is the quickest and easiest way to set yourself on the right path, especially when it comes to meeting your longer-term goals. It's what we call "smart goal-setting". By employing six or seven weekly goals, you're ensuring that you get somewhere fast, while encouraging yourself along the way.

One week goals might include:

- Writing a paper.
- Doing all of your homework.
- Reading a book.
- Posting on your blog.
- Going to your therapy session.
- Trying a new coping method.
- Going to the gym at least twice.
- Having dinner with your parents.

Do you see how well your "base goals" transition into little chunks? Going to the gym can help your physical appearance, doing your homework can help with your education, having dinner with your parents can improve your family relationships, and going to your therapy session can improve your mental health.

One Month

In general, you should have twice the amount of monthly goals as you would in a single week. So, basically, two weeks' worth of goals. At the end of thirty days, you're going to be able to accomplish more than you did each week, by adding up the collection of four weeks. The nice thing about "longer" terms is that you don't have to actually work for them. You use them to measure how well you're setting your "shorter" terms. For example:

- Paying all of your bills.
- Saving at least $100.
- Attending three sessions of therapy.
- Losing five pounds.
- Buying two new outfits.
- Taking your partner on three nice dates.
- Cleaning and organizing your apartment.

These might seem a bit overwhelming because of their size. That's why you break them down into smaller chunks to accomplish each week. Maybe one week you clean the kitchen, the next week you go through your storage unit, and so on. Make it manageable. You'd be shocked at what you can accomplish.

Three Months

I can't even begin to tell you how many people underestimate what they can do in three months, just by setting little goals each week and bigger goals each month. Slowly but surely, they take a big step toward their "base goals".

Weekly and monthly goals are necessary to properly measure how far you've come. But three month goals are a way of checking in. They tell you whether or not you need to push harder, or take a step back. This is around the time when you should start asking yourself, "How have I felt during this process?"

These goals might include:

- Improving my mental health by a numerical level of 2.

- Saving over $500 for the future.
- Improving my relationship by a numerical level of 3.
- Fully organizing my apartment and my place of work.
- Reading ten books and subscribing to a magazine.
- Doing all of my homework and maintain good grades.

You can see how these little goals start to snowball. At this point, we're talking about "significant" goals, rather than short term goals. This continues at the six month level.

Six Months

After six months, you're pretty set in your ways. There's an awful lot you've been able to accomplish by now, but there's still a long way to go. By this point in time, you should feel satisfied with the work that you've done. It might be time to set some new goals and eliminate a few that you've sufficiently improved upon.

Some six month goals could be:

- Losing thirty pounds.
- Saving over $2,000.
- Moving out of my parents' house.
- Limiting my therapy appointments to an as-needed basis.
- Finding a coping method that truly works for me.
- Passing all of my classes with B's or above.
- Reading twenty books.

Again, people underestimate how much they can do in a limited time span, and they end up regretting it later. They don't try enough when it counts, because they don't think that it's possible. But the truth of the matter is, all of your goals tie into one another. They mesh, in a strong and tangible way. Your annual goals are no different.

One Year

Here, we're stepping over the boundary between "significant" goals and long term goals. You're going to start accomplishing your broad goals at this point, based on how far you've come since you started measuring and maintaining your goal schedule. Those weeks add up.

These goals might include:

- Improving my overall relationship with my parents.
- Feeling healthier than I did last year.
- Losing fifty pounds.
- Saving over $5,000 for my future.
- Finding a new job that makes me happy.
- Leaving my miserable relationship.
- Learning how to fully cope with my anxiety.
- Learning how to let go of my past.
- Making better friendships.
- Making better choices.

And, just like that, your base goals have been accomplished. But where do we go from here?

Five Years

Believe it or not, the goal-setting process can span even longer than a year. Though more than 90% of your goals will most likely fit within that timeframe, some will hit this five year mark. You can't realistically expect yourself to accomplish specific feats in three hundred and sixty-five days. Sometimes, that just isn't enough.

For example:

- Graduating from college.
- Getting a big promotion.
- Buying a house.
- Having my first child.
- Being financially stable.
- Getting married (or into a serious relationship).

- Adopting a pet from an animal shelter.
- Starting my own company.
- Making more than $20 an hour.

These can't happen overnight. In fact, they can't even happen within a year. But, by setting goals at the small level (and employing just a little bit of luck), you can reach them within five years. But what can you complete in ten?

Ten Years

Yes, there's more. Some goals are even bigger than five years. In fact, they span an entire decade. A good way to set these goals is by asking the question, "Where do I see myself in ten years?" Then, start asking yourself for the things that you need to get there. For instance:

- Put my kids through college.
- Purchase a hybrid car.
- Visit Paris.
- Go to Hawaii.
- Make a difference in my community.
- Run for public office.
- Graduate and receive my Master's degree.
- Retire using my 401K.

These goals can vary greatly, depending on where you are in your life when you make them. Some cater to younger individuals, just starting their lives. Others cater to older individuals, looking to wind down and enjoy their retirement. What are you looking to accomplish?

Lifetime Goals

And, of course, there are lifetime goals. There are things that you can't put a timestamp on, no matter how hard you try. The most popular of these goals include:

- Changing the world.

- Becoming President.
- Visiting all fifty states.
- Moving to Canada.
- Owning a horse.
- Renovating a home.

There are dozens of other ideas, in addition to the ones presented here. But this should be enough to help you grasp the concept of a lifetime goal. Everyone has at least one. What's yours?

Your Action Task

We're getting down to the wire here. It's almost time to start setting our goals. But, before you can do that, you need to obtain the answers to a few simple questions.

- Do you picture yourself with more long term goals or more short term goals? Why? Do you think you would benefit from organizing yourself this way?
- Do you have many lifelong goals? Or do you still think of yourself as too young for them?
- Do you have many "significant" goals? Where do most of your timelines fall?

You need to really think about these this while you have the chance because, once we get to the real stuff, I won't have as much advice for you. This is all going to be focused on your wants and yours needs, so we can lead into topics like accountability and evaluating your goals thus far.

Ready?

Let's get to it.

Step 5: Set Your Goals

The time has finally come to get started with the goal-setting process. As a quick review for you:

- We've talked about determining your needs. These needs should be based in at least three of the ten suggested categories, including: physical traits, emotional stability, mental health, financial assistance, employment opportunities, romantic relationships, friendships, family issues, contribution needs, education, and organization.

- From these needs, you should have been able to create a set of broad goals. We gave examples of these goals in section three. They are usually six month, one year, five year, ten year, or lifelong when it comes to their length.

- We also talked about different ways to create your goals. For the purpose of this section, we're going to suggest that you remain SMART in your decisions (specific, measurable, achievable, realistic, and time-bound). In other words, make your goals revolve around something that you can measure, be realistic about your ability to reach your goals, and set a timeline for just about everything. We highly suggest that you write down your goals, as well.

- Finally, we had an in-depth discussion about timelines. You should know the difference and the purpose of each section. At this point in time, you should be prepared to set your own goals.

While you're thinking about your future, your present, and your decisions, we're going to have a talk about performance goals and outcome goals (as well as realistic goals and unrealistic goals). I find that these topics are often important to those who are new to the goal-setting process.

41

Performance Goals vs. Outcome Goals

In the process of setting healthy goals, you need to be fair to yourself. Setting performance goals, rather than outcome goals, can help you achieve that.

Why? Because one of them measures your success by what changes around you (which you can't control) and one of them measures your success by what you change yourself (which you can control). There is an obvious advantage to using one over the other, because you aren't holding yourself accountable for things beyond your reach.

You can't necessarily change the world without some help. You can't blame yourself if other people don't follow your lead. But you can change yourself and your surroundings with your actions. Thus, we have performance goals versus outcome goals.

Performance Goals

These goals are based entirely upon you and what you're capable of doing. They are measured by your actions, your talents, and your work. Some examples of performance goals include:

- I want to be more productive at work.
- I want to write my English paper.
- I want to finish my homework.
- I want to learn how to play the piano.
- I want to renew my driver's license.
- I want to graduate from college.
- I want to do my best in my job interview.
- I want to make a great resume.

These are all achievable goals, based solely on the fact that you're able to complete them without any outside help. You know what you want, and you're able to do it for yourself. That makes these goals positive, realistic, timely, and (pretty much) awesome. They're all about you. That's what you're looking for in a good goal set.

They also help you move forward in your focus areas, because they change the way you work for things and the way you see things. They help you understand what you're possibilities are, and where your potential lies. If the outside world rewards you for it, so much the better. I highly suggest that the majority of your goals are performance goals, if not all of them.

You can't make the world revolve around your new way of seeing life. But you can make your life change by altering your thoughts, desires, and actions. That's what performance goals are all about. What can *you* do to improve your situation?

Outcome Goals

These goals are based on the world around you, and what may or may not change because of your decisions. The problem with outcome goals is that they are measured by what changes are made in your surroundings, rather than by what you've done yourself. For example:

- I want to get a promotion.
- I want to receive an award.
- I want to win the lottery.
- I want to get the job.
- I want to be cast as the lead in a musical.
- I want to be chosen to represent my school.
- I want to win the debate.
- I want my professor to like me.
- I want my boss to like me.

These are all things that you can't make happen, no matter what you do. You can want the job, but that doesn't mean you'll be chosen. You can want a promotion, but that doesn't mean you're going to be given one. You can want to win the lottery, but that's not something you can control. It's left up to chance. It's left up to someone or something else that you can't influence. That's the problem with outcome goals. They sound good, at first. But they're more like bucket list items. You'd like for it to happen to you, and you might have even done something to push the process along, but it didn't happen solely because you worked for it.

This can be unfair to the goal-setter, because if they fail, it isn't really their fault.

Realistic Goals vs. Unrealistic Goals

We need to talk now about setting realistic goals. I promised we'd have a section on this, and there's a very real reason why.

Too many times in the past, I've seen new goal-setters make the mistake of pushing themselves too hard too soon. They find that they can't even meet their weekly goals, because they're expecting so much from themselves. They struggle each and every day to fight but, eventually, they give up. They decide that setting goals is just too difficult, and not really worth it.

This isn't how it should feel to have goals. It should feel natural. Comfortable, even. It should feel like you're accomplishing more than you ever thought you could have. You should always be impressed with yourself during this process; not let down. That's how you know you're doing something right.

Realistic goals should make up the entirety of your list. You should never have a goal that's impossible to meet, or too demanding. Here's how you can tell that a goal is realistic:

- It has a reasonable turn-around time. You're not expecting yourself to write a paper in six hours, or change your entire life by the end of the year. You're doing something that you know is possible, such as finishing your homework for the week or starting your own business throughout the next decade.
- It has a reasonable about of work. You aren't pushing for sixteen pages by the end of the night. You aren't pushing to make $40,000 a month. Instead, you're setting your goals for just the right amount of effort. You want to write four pages. You want make $4,000 a month. Be real.

44

- It's something that you would expect from someone else. If your friend couldn't do it (or someone who has a skill set similar to yours couldn't do it), you shouldn't expect it from yourself. We make the mistake of assuming that, if we worked as much as we possibly could, we would be rich and well-off. But we're also human. And we can only do much before we explode.

- You've been able to do it before. You aren't trying to accomplish an incredible feat that you've never touched before in your life. You're expecting something from yourself that you've already proven you're capable of doing. For example, I wouldn't expect myself to be able to write twenty pages of content every single week. I'm not a writer, and I would never be able to meet a deadline like that.

Your Action Task

I'm pretty sure that you already know what's coming next. This is your time to sit down and write out your goals. Create a spreadsheet, if you want. Write them on lined paper, if you want. Illustrate them on computer paper, if that's easiest for you. No matter what method you choose to utilize, this is your opportunity to get everything out on paper.

I want you to explore and try to meet these goals for the next week. In theory, you should come back to the second half of this book fully prepared to start measuring, troubleshooting, and changing your goals.

That's where the sixth step will come into play. When you need a reminder of your own accountability.

Step 6: Stay Accountable

If you took my advice and waited about a week to start this section of the book, congratulations! You've make it through your first week of goal-setting. How did it feel? What have you managed to accomplish? Are you already starting to feel better about yourself and your future?

Right about now, you should be starting to feel a little sense of panic. You've made it through the beginning stages, but you're nervous about what you've been able to do and what you haven't been able to do. After all, the odds that you met all of your ambitious goals on the first week are slim to none. And that's okay. Because that's how you're going to learn.

If you didn't wait, that's alright. We're going to spend this section talking about staying accountable for your goals and remembering that, if you set them correctly, there's no reason why you shouldn't be able to succeed. You don't necessarily need to be far along in the process when you get this lecture. But it's usually a good reminder to those who are struggling.

Staying accountable is the key to meeting your goals. Refusing to make excuses, reminding yourself that only you have the power to say no, continuing to set realistic goals...all of these things have an effect on the outcome of your attempt to improve your life.

Share Your Goals

I pointed this out in an earlier step, and I'm going to continue to insist upon it. Sharing your goals with other people is the quickest and best way to ensure that you don't give up on yourself before you've even gotten started. Those around you will hold you personally responsible if you fail, and they'll have a harder time trusting you the next time that you insist you're trying to change. They've seen it and heard it already, and you didn't do it. That's going to make them lose interest.

And you, of course, don't want that. You want to impress the people around you, and prove to them that you're capable of making major differences in your focus sections. You can become the CEO of a company. You can save more than $5,000 a year. You can do everything and anything you say you're going to do; and that starts with telling the people around you. Then, it becomes an expectation.

Focus

No matter what might be going on in your life, don't lose sight of what you're fighting for. Even if you've gone through a bad breakup, lost your best friend, or had a major setback in your mental health, refuse to let that break you down. Deal with the problem, of course. But keep your focus on improving yourself. This strength is necessary to maintaining a steady structure of goals, because there's always going to be something that wants to get in the way. If you let it, you're making excuses for yourself and you're hurting your chances of real change.

Remember That Your Goals Are Attainable

This is probably one of the most important things you can read right now. Your goals are possible. Your goals are realistic. You specifically set them to be that way, right? The whole point was to create a series of steps to your future; small, achievable steps that add up to the big picture. As long as you did that, you're in a great place. Because, whenever you have doubts, you can remind yourself that you made realistic goals. You made goals that are possible to meet. And there's no excuse (and no reason) for you to not meet them.

I find far too often that, instead of accepting accountability and responsibility for their success or failure, new goal-setters tend to give up. They think, if they can't do it now, they can't do it at all. And that's such a shame to watch. It's miserable. Don't be that person. Your goals are possible. You determined that yourself.

47

Remember That You Have Power

Empower yourself. You are incredible. You've made it this far (and you purchased this book) because you have the ability to meet whatever goal you set. You know that. And, if you can't meet the goal, you have the power to change it. You have the power to alter your expectations. You have the power to sit down and work, or get up and play. You get to make these choices. You can walk away from this program whenever you want. But you're still here. Why? Because that's your decision. And that's what you want for yourself. And you have the power.

Always Be Realistic

Never give up on the idea of being smart about your goal-setting strategy. Always think as clearly as you possibly can. If a goal seems like it's just too hard to meet, troubleshoot it or change it. Make a new goal altogether. If a turn-around time seems like it needs to be extended, go ahead and extend it. You aren't here to kill yourself; you're here to improve yourself. And you get to call the shots. If you feel like you're going to lose your mind if you continue pushing yourself, take a step back. It's not hurting anyone, and it's saving you.

This isn't like exercise. You're not trying to push yourself until your covered with sweat, can't breathe, and desperately need a shower. You're just going to push yourself until you feel a strain. You shouldn't feel that kind of strain at all. You should just feel a sense of motivation and strength. That strain means you're doing something wrong; you're expecting too much from yourself. You're still human. That's not going to change.

Your Action Task

Write down any goals that you've struggled to meet over the past week (or since you last picked up this book). In the next chapter, we're going to talk about how to properly measure your goals, as well as how to evaluate your process.

Using this information, we're going to separate the "good" goals from the "bad goals", and we're going to alter your methods (just a bit). This is our checks-

and-balances system. Together, we're going to make a real, working regimen for you. It just involves a bit of editing, a little technical knowledge, and a lot of self-determination.

And one last tip before we continue. Go back through the first four chapters and see how well your goals match up with them. What have you been doing correctly? What have you been doing incorrectly? Throughout the next several steps, this is going to matter greatly.

Step 7: Review and Evaluate Your Goals

At this point, you should have a list of goals that you're struggling to meet. Or else, you should have a list of goals that you really want to evaluate or measure, based on what you've been experiencing.

One of the biggest things that I learned when I was just starting out in this field is that making your goals is only half of the process. If I turned you loose at this point, you'd miss a lot of important information about how to take your previous goals and make them that much better.

It's unrealistic to think that, the first time you set your goals, you've done enough. It's wrong to think that you're never going to have to touch them again. I promise, you will. And it's not going to make you happy. In fact, it's probably going to be frustrating. When you made your original goals, you had this image of what the first week (or month) was going to look like.

Some of you have probably come close to that image; others have probably failed miserably. It all depends on the expectations that you had for yourself when you created your goals. If those were too high, there's no sense in keeping what you've made. You're going to need to alter it, at least a little bit. If your expectations were too low, you're going to have to raise the bar.

In this step, we're going to discuss how to track your goals, what questions you should ask yourself about your goals, how to measure your progress, and how to determine when goals have become problems (or completely unattainable). That should lead directly into our troubleshooting phase.

Tracking Your Goals

It's not easy to determine how far you've come without the proper tools for measurement. If you wanted to spend six hours each week studying for your anatomy class, you're going to need to write down those hours somewhere. You're going to need to keep track somehow. The same goes for situations in which you need to measure money, time, effort, or improvement. There are different scales for all of these things, which we'll discuss in just a few moments.

Questions You Need To Ask

In order to fully understand whether or not a goal is positively affecting your present and your future, you need to ask yourself the following questions:

- Am I enjoying my experience with this goal?
- Do I feel that this goal is important to my future?
- Are there other goals that come first and/or could take over this goal?
- Is this goal realistic? Am I kidding myself by thinking that I can do it?
- How do I honestly feel about this goal?
- If I could go back, would I keep this goal on my list?
- Could the turn-around time on this goal be edited to make it more realistic?

Measurements and Outcomes

After you've asked these questions, you need to begin measuring the goal to see how much progress you've made. Below are some popular examples of measuring units.

- Time – This applies for goals that require you to do things such as write a paper in two days, read a book in three days, or take a test in sixty minutes.
- Money – This applies for goals that require you to do things such as save money, spend wisely, earn money, or pay employees.
- Effort – This measurement is a little less straightforward. It applies for goals such as doing well at work, giving something your full attention, or staying off of your phone. It's usually measured on a scale of 1-10.

- Improvement – Again, this measurement is a bit more difficult to account for. It applies for things such as improving coping methods, lowering anxiety attacks, and handling panic attacks. It's usually measured on a scale of 1-10.

When Goals Become Problems

Let's be real. At some point in time, you're going to have a goal that just isn't working for you. And again, that's completely okay. We can be unrealistic sometimes when we set our goals. Often, we don't know what kind of issues we might face. We don't know what our circumstances are going to be. That all being said, it's best to take a goal off of the board when it starts to become a real problem. That's when you start troubleshooting and making changes.

However, the real question is, how to you determine when a goal has become a problem? There's sort of a step-by-step process that goes with this. Almost like a sub-series of chapters that you need to follow. I'll outline them for you here.

1. The Discovery

This is when the alarm goes off in your head. This is when you realize something isn't right about a particular goal. For the purpose of this outline, let's say that you want to go the gym four times a week. Okay. That's a perfectly normal goal. It's realistic. It's obtainable. You even have a set of exercises that you're required to do while you're there. At first glance, there's nothing wrong here.

But life gets in the way. You've been given extra hours at work. You're exhausted at night. You feel sick when you exercise in the morning. You're trying to find a way to accomplish this goal without making yourself go crazy. And that's when the alarm bell starts sounding. Something here isn't right.

2. The Measurement

At this point, you need to continue trying to reach your goal for at least a week. I would try for two, if possible. Sometimes, you'll discover that life will step aside for your goals, and you'll be able to make time. Other times, there won't be a way out and you'll be stuck. The measurement process is there to help you make that determination. It's almost like a trial period. You're saying alright, I'm going to give this a fair shot. And if it doesn't work, I'm going to walk away.

3. Removal

Here, you've made it past the measurement stage and it still just isn't working. You're killing yourself trying to continually reach this goal, and you don't find it realistic anymore. Something has changed, or something was unaccounted for, and now you're stuck with something that you can't do.

While I always suggest that you give your goals a fair chance (if they were developed correctly), I don't suggest that you continue giving yourself a hard time. This is normal, and it happens. Especially in the beginning. So at this point, you need to remove yourself from the problem. This is when the goal moves to troubleshooting, where you can determine what exactly the issue is going to be and how you can fix it.

Your Action Task

Follow this process for any goals that are continually giving you a problem. This might take a couple weeks, and that's okay. When you're done, come back to the troubleshooting section with any written goals that aren't working.

We'll talk you through troubleshooting at that time.

Step 8: Troubleshoot Your Goals

At this time, you'll need to collect any information you have on goals that didn't work out for you. Before you decide to get rid of them forever, we're going to discuss troubleshooting, and how to get rid of some popular barriers that can get in the way of goal completion. If, at the end of this segment, your goals still aren't solved and you don't think there's any realistic way of changing them, you can scrap them and start over.

However, if you feel that there's still a chance and you want to keep trying, take those goals to the next step. There, we'll discuss how to change your goals and create new ones, based off of the ideas you developed in your original goal-setting process.

Troubleshooting is a difficult step, because it involves critical thinking. You need to sit down and try to determine what is stopping you from achieving your goal. It seems realistic. You don't see any reason why you should be struggling. Yet, you just can't do it. That doesn't make you weak or wrong. It means that something else is getting in the way. And it's your job to figure out what that is, so that it can be eradicated in the future.

Chances are, if something is affecting at least one of your goals, it has the potential to affect more. And that turns into one great, big mess. That stops you from meeting your broad goals. It stops you from improving. It's a slippery slope. I always suggest that, when something just isn't working out, you put it through the troubleshooting process and try to save it. That can help you with other problems in the future, and it will assist you in better managing your initial goal-setting.

Popular Barriers

When it comes to each, individual category, there are certain things that can get in the way of improvement. Here, we've collected those popular barriers.

We're going to talk about what causes each one, and how you can overcome them.

Sometimes, troubleshooting involves setting even more goals to eliminate underlying problems. That's something you're going to have to get used to doing. As I learned when I was starting out, the goal-setting process is a cycle. It never truly ends.

Sleep Deprivation

This problem can affect the vast majority of categories. If you're trying to improve your physical health, sleep deprivation can stop you from exercising. If you're trying to work at home, sleep deprivation can force you into endless naps and the need to close your eyes. Your emotional stability and mental health can both be affected, as well as your employment opportunities and the decisions that you make financially. All kinds of relationships can be damaged, including friendships and family ties. Your education can certainly be hurt by a lack of sleep. Basically, this is the holy grail of all barriers. And you need to solve it as soon as possible if it's proving to be a problem.

Hunger Pangs

This barrier mostly affects those who are trying to improve their physical health, which is usually a struggle to begin with. Hunger pangs can be caused by a number of things, but it mostly boils down to eating an unhealthy diet and lacking proper exercise. It can also affect you financially, because you'll spend money to eat fast and avoid cooking. Hunger pangs drag you down a lot more than you'll realize, at first. Then, when your credit card bill comes in and you see how much money you've spent at fast food restaurants and the grocery store, you'll be hit with an unwelcomed epiphany. Fortunately, hunger pangs are fairly simple to get rid of, which we'll talk about in a few sections.

Withdrawals

I wouldn't expect this barrier to hurt relationships or your education, in particular. But it's going to affect your ability to quit whatever it is that you're trying to quit. You might be having withdrawals from a lack of cigarettes, drugs, alcohol, or food. It could be much simpler than that. Maybe you're having withdrawals from a lack of romance, your family, or a very important friend. But, in this instance, we're discussing withdrawals that cause you to shake, pass out, or drool. This is a medical problem, and it very often gets in the way of goals set to eliminate a dangerous substance from your life.

Communication

Relationships are hurt by this barrier constantly. I can't tell you how many times I've seen couples break up, friends part ways, and families fall apart because of communication problems. People sometimes don't know what to say or how to feel, so they fail to properly explain their actions. Text messages have made everything worse, because cell phones and simple text lack character and context. We could have the same conversation in person, and no one would get angry. To overcome this barrier, you'll need the help of others. But there are quite a few options you can try.

Outside Interference

There's nothing you can do about this barrier. I'm going to tell you that right now. If you set outcome goals rather than performance goals, I guarantee this barrier is why you're reading this section; because outside forces have caused you to "fail" reaching your goal. It could also be because a hurricane hit your neighbourhood, your gym closed down, or a family member died. Sometimes, something will get in the way. The best thing you can do, when a goal falls into this abyss, is try to find a way around the problem, or set your sights on another focus point (for now).

Unrealistic Goal Setting

Maybe you've gone through the troubleshooting process and the only thing you've been able to determine is that your goal wasn't realistic in the first place. Maybe you knew that going in. Maybe you didn't. Either way, you're here now, and there's nothing you can do to meet this goal. At this point, you need to make a change or try a different tactic. Unfortunately, you might have to drop the goal altogether, if it's already too late to reach it. This is why setting realistic goals is so important from the get-go. Remember that, from now on.

Popular Solutions

For each barrier (generally), there is a solution. This could be anything from seeing a specialist to eating a healthier diet. At the end of the day, the only way you are ever going to be able to reach all of your goals is if you get rid of the factors that continually get in your way. Withdrawals aren't going to stop anytime soon. Sleep deprivation can be a decade-long problem. Communication isn't going to fix itself. And all of these things are going to stop you from achieving your overall goal of change. They're going to stop you from improving. So, how do we begin to lower the consequences of these undeniable barriers?

Take Naps

Sleep deprivation is most easily solved by taking naps. Not long naps, but thirty-minute power naps. Of all nap lengths presented, these best benefit your body and allow you to be more focused throughout the day. When the feeling strikes you, set your alarm and shut your eyes. Contrary to popular belief, naps have been scientifically proven to improve your overall health. I wouldn't call that a waste of time. You can also improve your sleep cycle by going to bed earlier, speaking with a doctor about possible insomnia, or exercising more often (this makes it easier to sleep at night). You should also try to utilize your internal clocking. Waking up naturally is always healthier than waking up to an alarm clock.

Create Healthy Meal Plans

Solving your hunger pangs can be as simple as creating a healthy meal plan and exercising more often. Often times, we feel hungry at irregular intervals because we aren't eating three separate meals each day. When I was a teenager, I skipped breakfast, ate a huge lunch, and snacked throughout the day. Sometimes, I would make dinner just before I went to bed. This is bad for your body, because the food you've digested spends all night settling in your stomach. It has no time to burn off the extra calories. You should be eating three distinct meals per day, with healthy snacks in between. You'll feel more awake, more alert, and more prepared. And those hunger pangs will, within two weeks, disappear altogether.

Seek Help

If you're struggling to control withdrawals, you need to see a doctor as soon as possible. This also applies for other physical issues, or prolonged sleep deprivation. Getting help from a professional is a great way to eliminate an underlying problem that you can't solve yourself. It also isn't admitting defeat. It's recognizing that, even though you're trying to fix yourself, there can be problems that are outside your realm of control. You can't make withdrawals go away, but certain medications can help you through the process. You can't make insomnia disappear with naps alone, but certain methods presented by a specialist might be able to help shut your eyes for the night. I know it sounds like a difficult thing to do, but seeking help is the best choice you can make when you face a problem that you can't overcome.

Counseling

In the same way that certain problems require you to seek professional help, communication and mental health issues might require you to seek counseling. A therapist can help determine your areas of difficulty, and they can work with you on an individual basis to improve in those areas. A therapist is going to help you achieve your goals, and is covered by most insurance companies. I highly suggest seeking entry into a program nearby, if you're worried that you can't go through this process alone. I improved drastically after my time in counseling, and I don't seek myself as "crazy" or "unstable". I just needed someone to talk with. Maybe you do, too.

Change Tactics

If everything else fails, try going at it from a different angle. Maybe you can't go to the gym four times a week if you go after work. That's fine. What about doing yoga in the mornings before work? Sure, exercising itself makes you feel sick first thing in the morning. But nobody said anything about yoga. Two mornings a week, plus two evenings of exercise a week, equals four trips to the gym. By using this method, you can save your goals and make them more realistic, without having to admit defeat on them altogether.

Change Your Goal

Maybe you can't change tactics. Maybe you don't have time in the morning to do yoga before work. That's fine. You need to change your goal. There's nothing else for it. Now, you go to the gym three times a week. Or you go to the gym twice a week, and do some exercises at home twice a week. There's nothing saying you can only exercise in a designated area. Make it work anywhere you go. This is just a scratch on the surface when it comes to changing your goals, but we'll talk more about that in the next section.

Your Action Task

Troubleshoot your goals and determine which ones fall under which popular barriers. There are brief instructions in the introduction to this section that should help you. If your goal doesn't fit any of these parameters, or you just don't think you need it, you can scrap it and start over. If you have goals that need to be changed because outside factors are getting in the way or you made an unrealistic expectation for yourself, take them to the next section.

Step 9: Change Your Goals

Here, we're going to change any goals that aren't working for you. A popular barrier isn't getting in the way. There isn't anything you can do to change it. It's just too far gone to be saved. Alright. We're going to take that and turn it into something that you can actually use. We'll change the parameters to make it possible, or we'll scrap it and come up with something completely and totally new.

Whatever we end up doing, however, there's still one last lecture to be had. If you've brought more than six goals to this section, you're probably not being realistic about what you can do and what you can't do. That means we need to have another conversation about attainability and impossibility.

We also need to walk through some basic questions. You need to determine whether or not changing is actually necessary, you need to figure out what went wrong (and if you had anything to do with it), you need to figure out what you need to change, and you need to decide if the goal itself is necessary to your improvement. Maybe you didn't reach your goal because you didn't really think it was important. Maybe you didn't realize just how important it was. Either way, we'll talk about that.

Then, at the end, you'll be set loose to make the necessary changes to your goals. This time around, you need to make sure that you're doing it correctly. You'll always need to monitor and alter your goals, based on changes in your surroundings and how you've changed as a person. But, this early on in the process, you need to be as succinct as possible. Otherwise, you'll lose interest and give up. It's all about taking little things and turning them into something impossibly big. Some people lose sight of that by trying to bite off more than they can chew.

Attainability vs. Impossibility

So, what's possible and what isn't? How can you determine when your goals have gone too far, and when they haven't gone far enough? We've talked about this already, but I'm going to give you one last crash course in possible versus impossible, attainable versus unattainable, and (ultimately) attainability versus impossibility.

There are things you can do, and there are things you can't. And no amount of goal-setting is going to change that fact. The basics of goal-setting tell us that we can't expect too much from ourselves all at one time. That's why this particular rule is so important. Should you push for more from yourself? Of course. But it needs to be within reason.

Attainability

This is how you obtain that reason. You set your sights toward something not only attainable, but realistic. And yes, there's a difference between the two. You can attain a goal that says you want to write six papers in one day. But that doesn't mean your goal is realistic. And you have to be able to get both of those traits in one, specific goal. You need to be able to say, "Alright, I can do this and I'm going to be able to do this without going insane." If you can't say that about your goal, you're doing it wrong.

Usually, I would say that there's no wrong way to set a goal. But this situation is a bit different. While goals are structured according to your wants and needs, there are basic human rules of functionality that you can't escape. It's pretty simple. If you can't do it, don't set it.

Impossibility

Unfortunately, I see far more impossible goals being set by beginners than possible goals. They want to visit every country in the world, save $20,000 by the end of the year, buy their first house in three months, and get a promotion. There are numerous errors with these goals (outcome versus performance being one of the biggest), but hands down largest problem is the lack of attainability. Sure, you could write six papers in one day. That goal is attainable, but not realistic. But you can't visit every country in the world. At least, not without a lot of help and a stroke of luck. That's not attainable, and it's definitely not realistic.

It's also a form of an outcome goal. You can try all you want, but you probably can't visit North Korea. I'm sure you'd also have some trouble visiting places like Iraq or Syria. It just isn't something that you can expect from yourself. Getting a promotion is the same story, but on a smaller scale. Yes, it would be fantastic to make more money and have a better job description. But that doesn't make it possible for you to force it to happen.

Popular Questions

Attainability and a realistic frame of mind. These are two necessary things for a goal to be successful. But what else do you need? What happens when it comes to actually changing your goals? What can you do to improve yourself without expecting too much? How do you take an impossible goal, and somehow make it possible?

I'll give you an example from my teenage years. When I was seventeen, I wanted to buy my first car. I gave myself three months to do it, while saving money from my then-crappy job. I realized very quickly that my goal was impossible. I wasn't going to be able to get what I wanted out of it, no matter how hard I worked or how much I wanted to make it happen.

So, I decided that I needed to change my goal. I figured out what I was doing wrong. I expected a minimum wage position to earn enough money in three months to purchase a $3,000 vehicle. That wasn't attainable. Instead, I looked for alternative ways of earning money. I started freelancing, mowing lawns and house-sitting for my neighbors. I did extra work for my teachers. I also pushed my turn-around time to six months. The pressure was off of me, and I was able to focus on my work. Within five months, I had my car. Had I continued with my original goal, I would have given up and much of what you're reading probably wouldn't exist.

To get to this point, you need to ask yourself some important questions. Then, you can use the answers to solve the problem.

Is Changing Necessary?

Do I really need to change my goal to get what I want? If there's absolutely no other way for you to achieve your goal through other tactics, than the answer to this question is yes. I never would have been able to purchase a car by following my original outline. In that case, I had to make a change. Otherwise, it would never get done.

But let's try a different example. Let's say I wanted to finish all of my homework for the week before Friday evening, every week. I felt like it was impossible, so I decided to change it. However, I didn't stop to think about the fact that I spent Wednesday and Thursday nights watching movies with my friends. I realized, if I stopped doing that during the week and met with them on the weekends, I would be able to reach my goal.

What Went Wrong?

In the case of doing my homework, I was failing to prioritize my time. I spent weeknights with my friends, making it literally impossible to finish my work in time. By changing that fact, I was able to successfully complete my goal. I was able to adapt.

But, when it came to my first car, the problem was financial. I wasn't making enough money. In order to reach my goal, I needed to account for those problems and find a way to make my car more attainable. It wasn't a simple fix, or a matter of scheduling. I had to make some serious changes in my life.

It all depends on what exactly went wrong with your goal. If you're able to fix what went wrong, go for it. If you're not, you probably need to rethink your goal altogether. There are other ways that I could achieved my needs. If a bus could have gotten me to school or to work, that would have been enough. I could have found new ways to get to the heart of the problem. And that's how you sometimes have to look at it. You have to be creative. You have to problem-solve.

Is The Goal Necessary?

Maybe I want a $50 watch, and I've been saving up to buy that watch for almost a month. At the end of the month, I realize that my goal isn't attainable. I haven't saved enough money to do what I want to do. I've troubleshot my goal. I know that I didn't account for basic financial needs. And now, I want to find a way to change my goal.

But what I really need to be doing is dropping my goal altogether. It isn't necessary to my future. I don't need it to improve myself. I don't need it to survive. It's just something that I want and can't really have right now. Goals like this are fine, to an extent. But if they reach this point in the goal-setting process, you need to leave them on the cutting room floor. They aren't doing you any good, and they're just tearing away at your confidence.

Your Action Task

Your job now is to change any goals that you couldn't meet as they were originally written. You'll have to test them for a week or two, to determine whether or not the change was sufficient. If it was, you can continue following you new goal. If it wasn't, you'll need to come back to this section and try again. At that point, you should really consider whether or not the goal is right for you.

In our most important (and final) section, we're going to talk about how you can take action with your new goals.

Step 10: Take Action

This is the section that's really going to matter in the end. This is the section where we give you all of the tools and tips that you need to follow your goals and change your life.

It's been a long process. For some of you, this book has taken several weeks (or even a month) to pour through. And the journey that you're about to embark upon is even longer, and potentially more difficult. You'll need to refer back to this book, I'm sure. You'll need to try new methods and experiments with your possibilities. You'll need to be more realistic about what you can and can't do.

But, once you've managed to make all of those things happen, you're going to be looking a whole new world. This is a world where you can do just about anything. And, by setting weekly goals and slowly working your way toward the finish line, you'll come leaps and bounds from where you were before. You'll wonder why you didn't always live your life this way.

I'm getting older. It's been years since I created this step-by-step process, and even longer since I needed it the most. But I still use it. Each and every single day, I sit down in front of my goal board and I check off everything that I've managed to accomplish. Some of them are daily, some of them are weekly, some of them are monthly; but I'm knocking it out of the park. The point is, you don't have to stop. You don't ever have to stop.

What else can you do to ensure that you complete your goals?

Write Them Down

The more you keep track of your goals, the better off you're going to be. I can't even begin to tell you how many times I tried to go electronic and avoid writing my goals down on my white board. But it just doesn't feel the same. That satisfaction isn't there, when I'm able to check off every single weekly goal that I made for myself. It also isn't as easy to make new goals each week. I don't know where my basis is.

So, that means you should probably go out and buy a white board. Get lots of colors. Allow yourself some creativity and organization. You'll be surprised how quickly it grows on you. I couldn't survive without my goal board now. I would go insane. If that isn't your style, though, you can always type up your goals electronically or keep them in a notebook. Anything that tracks what you've created is good enough.

Talk Through Your Problems

You're going to struggle, and that's normal. Nothing about this is a simple process. If you find that you aren't meeting many of your goals and you just can't find that motivation, try talking to someone about it. It's okay to let them know that you feel like you're failing, and you're not sure what to do. If that doesn't work for you, try talking to yourself. I find that pacing my bedroom and talking myself through my problems is one of the most calming things I can do. Hearing my own voice say that it's going to be okay is more relaxing than hearing someone else say the same thing. That's just how I work.

But a best friend is also good for this part of the process. They can listen to you, and help you determine what you need to alter in order to make your goals work. In the end, the people around you care about you the most. And they're only going to encourage you to get better. By opening up about your concerns, you're essentially helping them do their job.

Refuse to Give Up

I'm sure you've heard someone tell you not to give up before. This is no different. However, it's extremely important that you don't give up during that first period of goal-setting.

You're going to have trouble keeping your head above water. You're going to feel overwhelmed and afraid. But just remember, if you give up during the first two weeks (and most people do), you're admitting defeat.

If you make it past two weeks, you'll be much more likely to follow and meet your goals. This is especially true once you've made changes to better fit your schedule and your capabilities.

Focus on the Future

When you go through a rough patch, focus on what's coming your way. I would have gone crazy when I was a teenager, if I just thought about how much my life sucked at the time. I had to keep thinking about my business. I had to keep dreaming about the future. It was the only thing that kept me alive. It was the only thing that kept me pushing every single day, even when meeting my goals seemed like the farthest thing from possible.

You just have to refuse to let it get to you. You have to create an image of what you want to get out of your goal-setting experience, and you have to push to paint that picture for yourself. It's never going to be perfect. But, by focusing on the future, you're keeping your angry thoughts at bay. You're keeping yourself going. And that's what you need more than anything at the beginning of your transformation.

Celebrate Your Success

Don't be afraid to celebrate how far you've come. You'd be shocked at how many people just check off their goals and never look back. You need to take a moment to be proud of yourself. Go out for ice cream. Make a status about it. Let people compliment you and tell you that they're proud of you. Let yourself enjoy that moment, because that's what all of this is for. It's about showing the world that you're capable. It's about showing yourself that you're capable. If you can't take a step back and celebrate that, you're going to have a hard time continuing.

Be Confident and Proud

People might try to bring you down. So what? Be proud of who you are, and refuse to let other people stop you from trying to achieve your goals. You've worked too hard for this to let someone else ruin it. And don't get in your own way! You might feel weak. You might feel like you can't do it. But don't let it show. This is going to be frustrating, but you need to fight like a warrior. You chose to set these goals for a reason. They don't know that reason, and you can't erase it. It's always going to be there. And that's one more reason to keep going. You know that you're strong enough, or you wouldn't have set these goals for yourself. Have as much belief in yourself along the way, as you did when you set your milestones.

Make More Milestones

You can't realistically improve your life if you don't continue to process of setting goals. It's just impossible. Even if you meet the first week's goals, or the first month's goals, it still isn't enough. You need to continue pushing until you can't anymore. If you keep meeting all of your goals, set up more to knock them down. Refuse to stop. That's what I did. And I'm still setting goals, even today. The more you try, the more you'll succeed. I remembered that when I was a teenager, and now I make more money than I ever could have imagined possible. You can do the same thing. You have to believe that, and understand it.

Keep a Planner

I wish I could emphasize how important it is to write down your thoughts, your goals, and your actions. I got a planner about six months into my goal-setting process, and I've never looked back. I absolutely love the fact that I can see, on a calendar, what I'm doing and how I'm improving. If you take anything away from this section, take this away. Go out to Staples or Walmart or wherever you do your shopping, and buy a planner.

Stay Organized

Building from that point, you should always stay organized. Get a filing cabinet, print out your records, and keep track of how far you've come.

Organization is the key to success when it comes to making new goals for yourself. Improving your life is all about how much you're willing to record and understand and measure about yourself. I'm telling you, the biggest thing I changed in my life was how I presented myself and how I kept myself organized. It's really the trunk of the tree. Everything builds from it. Finances, communication, relationships, education, job opportunities. They all stem from this basic plot point. You need to be organized.

That might involve investing some money into this process. That might involve taking a few risks. But they're going to pay off. It could be time consuming. It could discourage you sometimes. I promise you, though, you'll regret it if you don't keep everything straight.

Your Action Task

We've talked about everything. We've seen everything. We've done everything. Now, it's up to you to maintain the success rate of your goals. It's up to you to continue making new milestones, pushing yourself, and improving your life. It's up to you, because I've taught you everything that I know. I've given you all of the tools that I had, when I was starting out. And I'm excited to see what you can make of it.

Good luck out there.

-Brad

Summary

For your sake, let's do a small review of what we're learned over the course of this book.

Step 1: Determine Your Needs

In this step, I introduced you to popular areas of improvement. Those areas include physical traits, emotional stability, mental health, financial assistance, employment opportunities, romantic relationships, friendships, family issues, contribution needs, education, and organization. At the end of the chapter, you were asked to choose at least three goal areas for yourself.

Step 2: Choose A Goal Setting Method

In this step, we talked about popular goal-setting methods, such as SMART Goals, the Zig Ziglar Formula, the One Minute Approach, and the Agile Approach. I also introduced you to important goal-setting tips, such as setting priorities, making each goal positive, making measureable goals, keeping a timeframe in mind, being clear and precise, writing goals down, and being realistic. At the end of the chapter, you were asked to choose a goal method that stood out to you.

Step 3: Clarify Your Desires

In this step, we talked about your "broad goals" for this process. I gave examples of goals for each of the ten categories provided in the first step. At the end of the chapter, you were asked to create a list of goals that you wanted to meet; these were meant to be your "finish lines".

Step 4: Create Timelines

In this step, we talked about creating timelines, and how they differ from one another. We touched on the difference between long term goals and short term goals. We also discussed how to set one week, one month, three month, six month, one year, five year, ten year, and lifelong goals. At the end of the chapter, you were asked to determine where most of your needs fit. You were given a list of questions to answer.

Step 5: Set Your Goals

In this step, we took the time to set our goals. We talked about performance goals and outcome goals, as well as realistic and unrealistic goals. At the end of the chapter, you were asked to sit down and create your original goal list. You were also advised to spend a week working with this list to see how well you did.

Step 6: Stay Accountable

In this step, we discussed how you can stay accountable for your goals. We gave you tips, such as sharing your goals with friends and family, remembering that your goals are attainable, remembering that you have the power, and always being realistic. At the end of the chapter, you were asked to write down potential areas of weakness. You were told that we would use these in later chapters.

Step 7: Review and Evaluate Your Goals

In this step, we talked about reviewing and evaluating your goals. You were taught how to track goals, and what popular measurements to use. At the end of the chapter, you were asked to determine which of your goals had become unattainable. We decided to use these goals in the next step, in order to troubleshoot them.

Step 8: Troubleshoot Your Goals

In this step, we went through the lengthy process of troubleshooting our goals. We talked about popular barriers, such as sleep deprivation, hunger pangs, withdrawals, communication issues, outside inference, and unrealistic goal-setting. We also discussed popular solutions to these barriers, such as seeking help, taking naps, creating healthy meal plans, seeing a therapist, changing tactics, or changing your overall goal. At the end of the chapter, you were asked to troubleshoot your goals and bring any unresolved goals to the next step.

Step 9: Change Your Goals

In this step, we talked about changing your goals altogether. We focused on attainability versus impossibility, and knowing when your goals just aren't realistic. We also worked our way through questions, such as what went wrong with the goal, whether or not changing the goal was necessary, and what part of the goal could be changed to improve it. At the end of the chapter, you were asked to change your goals, and scrap any that just couldn't be altered.

Step 10: Take Action

In this step, we talked about taking action to pursue your goals. We gave you tips, such as writing down your goals, talking through your problems, refusing to give up, focusing on the future, celebrating your success, being confident and proud, continuing to track yourself, making more milestones, keeping a planner, and staying organized. At the end of the chapter, you were asked to continue pushing toward your goals. And I instructed you, as per usual, to never give up!

Now, go out there and change your life.

About the Author

Brad Jones is an internet marketer and digital entrepreneur. He now makes a 6 figure income by working online for myself running multiple businesses.

He started experimenting with earning money online back in 2002 on the side, whilst he continued working his 9-5 sales job. It wasn't until 2008 that he finally got to the point where his side income covered his monthly expenses, and he saw the opportunity to earn a lot more. He quit his job later that year and has been working for himself ever since.

Brads believes there are many people claiming how to make money online, and in his experience there is no ONE best way. He's found success in many avenues, and believes it's down to the individual's passions and interests that will produce the best results for them.

Brad has written several books demonstrating some of the ways you can make a living working online, and he's have found success in all of them.

"Be open to try new things, never quit, and you'll find the success you're looking for. I promise you!"

More Books by Brad Jones

Blogging Brilliance – How to A Make Bundle on Your Blog

Ebay Excellence – Making Easy Money the Ebay Way

Fiverr Freedom – From Your First Gig to Making A Fortune On Fiverr

Flawless Freelance Writing – How to Make A Fortune Freelance

Storytelling – A Storytelling System to Deliver Inspiring and Unforgettable Speeches

You're The Problem – 30 Real Life Solutions to Stop Destructive Actions and Get Out of Your Own Way

Social Media – The Ultimate Guide to Transforming Your Brand with Social Media

Business Ideas – The Ultimate Guide to Creating Innovative Business Ideas

Fiction Writing Templates – 30 Tips to Create Your Own Fiction Book

Non Fiction Writing Templates – 44 Tips to Create Your Own Non Fiction Book

www.ingramcontent.com/pod-product-compliance
Lightning Source LLC
Chambersburg PA
CBHW060415190526
45169CB00002B/910